# NEW ORLEANS
# CLASSICS

## B♭ CLARINET
## SOLO

**PLAYBACK+**
*Speed • Pitch • Balance • Loop*

To access audio visit:
**www.halleonard.com/mylibrary**

Enter Code
1675-2663-7579-9653

ISBN 978-1-59615-109-3

### Music Minus One

EXCLUSIVELY DISTRIBUTED BY

**HAL•LEONARD®**

Visit Hal Leonard Online at
**www.halleonard.com**

Contact us:
**Hal Leonard**
7777 West Bluemound Road
Milwaukee, WI 53213
Email: info@halleonard.com

In Europe, contact:
**Hal Leonard Europe Limited**
42 Wigmore Street
Marylebone, London, W1U 2RN
Email: info@halleonardeurope.com

In Australia, contact:
**Hal Leonard Australia Pty. Ltd.**
4 Lentara Court
Cheltenham, Victoria, 3192 Australia
Email: info@halleonard.com.au

# THE MUSIC

**Fidgety Feet** comes from the repertoire of the Original Dixieland Jazz Band. (Some say the individual strains were heard around New Orleans before the ODJB recorded the number in 1918.) The original title was "War Clouds," but "Fidgety Feet" is a better fit. The syncopations in the first strain conjure up images of eccentric dancing by Joe Frisco, or the Castles. Stoptimes on the second strain are often left open, though the drums fill in on this particular recording. The trio section is march-like and gives soloists a chance to improvise on a relatively uncomplicated melody.

**Tin Roof Blues** originated with another band of Crescent City expatriates—the New Orleans Rhythm Kings. First recorded in 1923, the number became part of the Dixieland repertoire almost immediately. It underwent some alterations in the 1950s and became a pop hit—with lyrics—called "Make Love to Me." The MMO version is played in the traditional style, including a "stop-three" (three beats and a rest on the fourth beat) behind the clarinet solo.

**Royal Garden Blues** celebrates the Chicago nightclub where King Oliver and His Creole Jazz Band played in the late 'teens and early '20s. It was copyrighted by New Orleans composers Clarence and Spencer Williams (they were not related) in 1919. Others have indicated that the tune was actually written by New Orleans clarinetist Jimmie Noone. Either way, it is an excellent vehicle for blowing. The breaks for the three horns in the second strain and the melodic line of the third section (B-flat Blues) are especially helpful in developing improvisational skills.

**Blue Orleans** is an original by Tim Laughlin. It has been recorded several times and given a variety of treatments. The arrangement for this session is in the contemporary blues style, with big band-like "hits" by the horns and rhythm. The clarinet is featured on this track, and those who play along will get a thorough blues workout.

**Dumaine Street Breakdown** is the second of three Tim Laughlin compositions included. The minor-key introduction recalls the verse of the New Orleans Rhythm Kings' "She's Cryin' for Me." The chorus is somewhat reminiscent of the Halfway House Orchestra's "New Orleans Shuffle." However, Tim's composition is not derivative; it just shares a common lineage with some outstanding homegrown New Orleans tunes.

**Savoy Blues** was composed by the quintessential New Orleans trombonist Edward "Kid" Ory. Ory recorded it for the first time with Louis Armstrong's Hot Five in 1927. The Bob Crosby Orchestra revived it in 1936. When Ory returned to the music business in the mid-1940s, he played the number frequently and made several new recordings of it. This version does not re-create the Hot Seven or Ory band recordings note-for-note. Still, most of the original melodic lines can be heard.

**March of the Uncle Bubbys** is Tim Laughlin's tribute to the old-timers in New Orleans who sit "on the banquet" in their "Esplanade shoits," drinking Dixie beer and talking in a dialect straight out of *A Confederacy of Dunces*. These characters love to "second-line" a Carnival parade, if the band plays the tempos favored by Pete Fountain's Half-Fast Walking Club. (This group includes Tim as a regular participant.)

**Do You Know What It Means to Miss New Orleans** is the only song in the program that was not composed by one or more New Orleans natives. It was written for the 1947 film *New Orleans*. That movie was dismal with regard to historical accuracy, but it allows us to see and hear Louis Armstrong, Papa Mutt Carey, Kid Ory, Barney Bigard, Bud Scott, Zutty Singleton and Billie Holiday onscreen! The song has become a standard in the Dixieland repertoire and is especially popular with tourists who enjoy live jazz in the city's nightclubs. The melody does capture the enchanting spirit of New Orleans that makes casual visitors long to return. Due to the slow tempo, on this recording the 32-bar choruses are divided in half between the soloists, rather than each musician taking a full chorus.

**Someday You'll Be Sorry** was composed by New Orleans' best-known musician: Louis Armstrong. Louis wrote this attractive melody in the late 1940s. He played and sang it with the All Stars for the rest of his life. As on the previous track, the solo choruses are split in 16-bar sections. The final solo is by the cornet, with the band taking the tune out at the halfway point—a typical Armstrong device.

**Quincy Street Stomp** is attributed to New Orleans soprano saxophonist Sidney Bechet. The first two strains are actually part of "Blame It on the Blues," a 1915 ragtime composition by Charles L. "Doc" Cook. (Cook wrote other rags before becoming a full-time bandleader. In the 1920s his orchestra featured several New Orleans musicians: Freddie Keppard, Jimmie Noone, Joe Poston, Johnny St. Cyr and Andrew Hilaire.) Bechet's original contribution to the piece is a march-like trio strain, similar to those heard in "Fidgety Feet" and "Chattanooga Stomp." Quincy Street in Brooklyn was where Bechet lived in the 1940s. Tim Laughlin and his musicians start the number with an old-time feel, then swing out on the trio.

*- Hal Smith*

3254

# CONTENTS

4

Bb Clarinet

# Fidgety Feet

Original Dixieland Jazz Band

6

Bb Clarinet

# Tin Roof Blues

New Orleans Rhythm Kings

MMO 3254

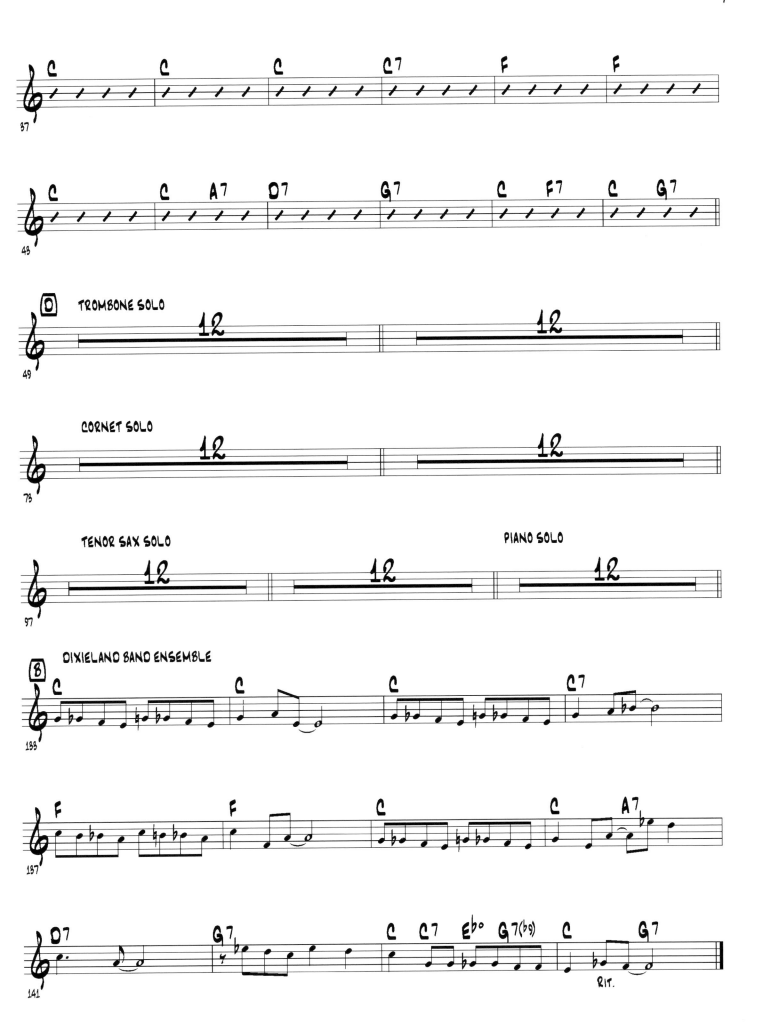

Bb Clarinet

# Royal Garden Blues

Clarence & Spencer Williams

# Blue Orleans

Tim Laughlin

14

Bb Clarinet

# Savoy Blues

Edward 'Kid' Ory

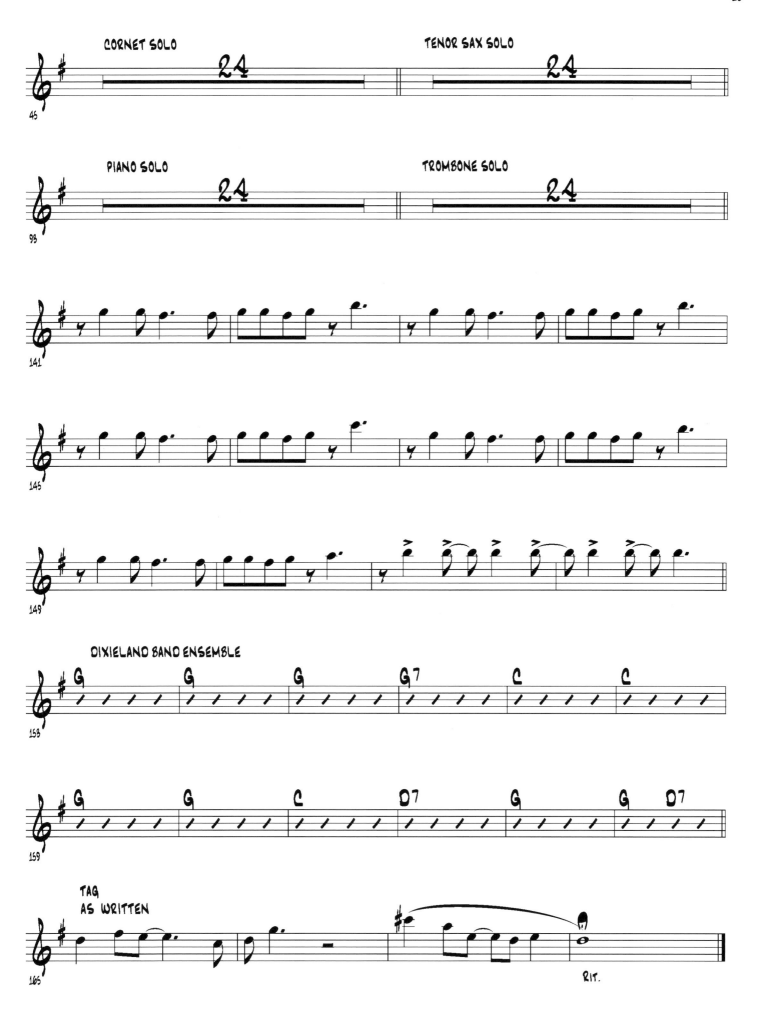

Bb Clarinet

# March of the Uncle Bubbys

Tim Laughlin

Bb Clarinet

# Do You Know What It Means to Miss New Orleans

Eddie DeLang
Louis Alter

Bb Clarinet

# Someday You'll Be Sorry

DIXIELAND BAND--ENSEMBLE ----FILL LIGHTLY

LOUIS ARMSTRONG

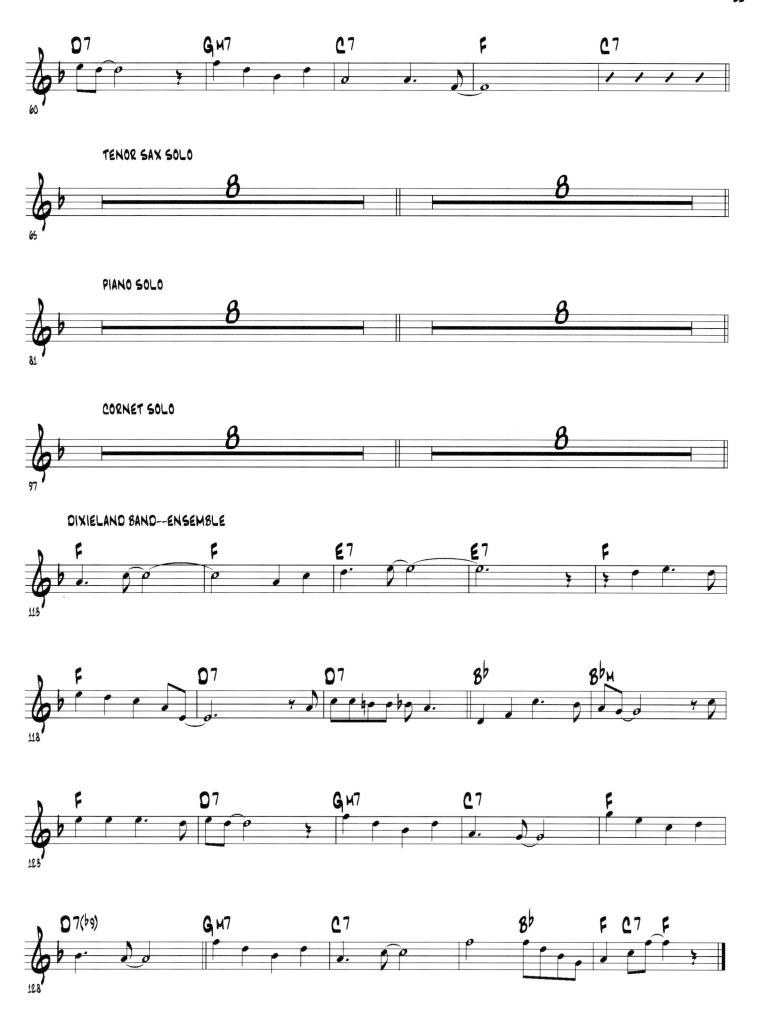

# Quincy Street Stomp

Sidney Bechet

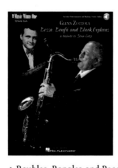